CAṄKAMA

teachings on
Walking Meditation

Most Venerable Uda Eriyagama Dhammajiva Maha Thero

Nissarana Vanaya, Mitirigala

Nissarana Vanaya - Mitirigala

Monks at Nissarana Vanaya on alms round

Stairway to Nissarana Vanaya Kuti

Table of Contents

Translator's Foreword	v
Editor's Testimonial	vii
Chapter One : Practicing Walking meditation	2
Chapter Two : Instructions on walking meditation	21
Chapter Three : Preparation of the Walking Path	31
Outdoor walking path	31
Indoor walking path	33
Chapter Four : Applying effort in Walking Meditation	36
Chapter Five : Q & A on Walking Meditation	55
Abbreviations	68

Translator's Foreword

Caṅkama (Walking Meditation) is a compilation of teachings on the subject by Most Venerable U Dhammajiva Maha Thero. These teachings have been adapted from several sources. The teachings included within *Sakman Bhāvanā* (Sinhala Publication 2007 - by Most Venerable U Dhammajiva Maha Thero) forms the core of the book. This book describes all aspects of walking meditation as part of the *Satipatthāna* practice and gives detailed instructions on the practice. During a meditation retreat at Nissarana Vanaya where Venerable Dhammajiva discussed the *Upawāna Sutta* (SN) he dealt extensively on this topic with reference to the *Viriya Sambojjhanga*. One Chapter in this book is devoted to those teachings mentioned. At every retreat, during the Dhamma discussions participants ask questions related to walking meditation. There is an attempt to capture some of those questions and related answers given by the Master, in this publication. A testimonial from the Editor of this book, who has strived to 'perfect' the art of walking meditation, has also been included. Finally, suggestions on how to construct walking paths or promenades, outdoors as well as indoors are also elaborated.

Most Venerable Dhammajiva Maha Thero is the Abbot and Chief Meditation Master of the forest monastery Nissarana Vanaya, Mitirigala in Sri Lanka. He has been teaching meditation practice for nearly twenty years. Regular participants at Venerable Dhammajiva's retreats have experienced the richness and lucidity with which he introduces the topic of walking meditation. The carefully constructed walking paths for male and female yogis, in addition to the walking paths included in every monk's hut or kuti in the upper monastery at Nissarana Vanya, bear testimony to the emphasis he places on this ancient practice. Constantly referring to the many hours devoted to walking meditation by the Buddha and his disciples from 2600 years ago, the Meditation Master reiterates that walking meditation, is one of the four equally important components of the practice, as taught in the *Satipatthāna sutta*.

In a typical retreat schedule at Nissarana Vanya and other retreat Centres where Venerable Dhammajiv*a* teaches, walking meditation and sitting meditation are given equal prominence. During a day of 10-12 hour intensive practice, fifty percent of the time is devoted to walking meditation. Students who had previously been exposed to teachings where sitting meditation formed the base of the practice, would experience a new dimension in their practice when attending retreats by this teacher. Not only do retreatants enjoy this component in the daily schedule of a retreat, but some meditators even experience deep insights during walking meditation.

The translator/transcriber is indebted to a fellow meditator for meticulous editing of this publication. The *Upawāna sutta* Dhamma talks were accessed on *http://www.damsara.org*, a valuable website which hosts most of Venerable Dhammajiva's teachings. A dedicated practitioner and student of this Master did the design and layout of this publication, and wished to remain anonymous.

Editor's Testimonial

A dear friend of mine initially introduced me to meditation and the introduction was to breath meditation or *ānāpānasati*. Living far away from home I had no access to a meditation teacher. I learnt from books and tried to watch my breath whenever I sat for meditation. A few years later I attended a one-day meditation retreat conducted by a visiting Sri Lankan monk. On that day I learnt the rudiments of walking meditation. But I did not give it the same importance as for sitting meditation and to watching my breath. To my good fortune (or good kamma), a Buddhist Temple was established by a Thai nun close to where I lived. Ever since then, I began visiting the temple once a week and commenced meditation under her guidance. This gave a great boost to my practice.

Walking meditation thus became a part of my routine. I would wake up daily at 5.00 AM with the idea of doing half an hour of walking and half an hour of sitting meditation before the rest of the household woke up. I would keep a timer for half an hour and start walking inside the house. Sitting meditation was not that much of a problem. But walking meditation was a different story!

As I started walking, my mind would be on the first few steps and then it would start to roam. It was a continuous stream of thoughts, jumping relentlessly from one topic to another and I wouldn't even be aware of it until the timer went off, signaling the end of the session. I would be mentally exhausted and frustrated with myself for not being able to "control" my thoughts. Although I would make a determination to do better the next day, again it would be the same. Feeling dreadfully cold during the winter mornings, I would wonder why, after making the effort to wake up so early that I couldn't make it work!

I had no idea what *Kamatahan* was. I had no idea that I should speak to my teacher about the difficulties I was having. What I did know was that I should not give up. So every day I would drag myself out of bed and start walking, walking, walking. This went on for about three years. Then one day without any warning, I found myself walking with my mind on my feet! With no thoughts cluttering my mind. I was delighted and found that it was the most sublime moment in my meditation practice. At that moment I knew that I had overcome a great obstacle. From that day onwards walking meditation became easier and something that I looked forward to immensely.

It is not to say that I had perfect mindfulness every time I practiced. No, it was the belief that I could bring back my mind to my feet even though the mind went astray. There were days that mindfulness was well established during most of the walking meditation session and there were days it wasn't that good.

Today, fifteen years later, I can say with 'pride' that I am well established in my practice of *sakman bhavana*, and that mindfulness gets established easily as soon as I commence the walking practice. And these walking meditation sessions give a tremendous boost to sitting meditation. For me it was simply the faith and confidence (*saddhā*), and the unrelenting effort (*viriya*) that helped me in my quest.

The editor practices meditation under the guidance of the Meditation Master, Most Venerable U Dhammajiva Maha Thero

Image credit SITHA NIVANA NISSARANA VANA ARANA, www.nissarana.lk

Monks walking mindfully

'Bhikkhus, there are these five benefits of walking meditation.
Which five?
One endures long journeys on foot.
One endures striving.
One enjoys better physical health.
Food and drink are digested well.
The samādhi generated from walking meditation is durable.

- *Cańkamānisaṁsa Sutta - AN 111 :29*

Chapter One

Practicing Walking meditation

Puna ca paraṃ bhikkhave, bhikkhū
Gacchanto vā gacchāmī'ti pajānāti
Ṭhito vā ṭhito'mhīti pajānāti
Nisinno vā nisinno mhīti pajānāti
Yathā yathā vā pan' assa kāyo paṇihito
Hoti tathā tathā naṃ pajānāti

(Iriyāpatha Pabbam – Mahā Satipatthāna sutta DN)

During the rains retreat at Nissarana Vanaya, the *sutta* used for discussion was the *Satipatthāna sutta* (DN and MN). I consider the *Satipatthāna sutta* as a key *sutta* that would help in developing meditation practice and in furthering the meditative life styles of us monastics at this monastery. In fact the Buddha said on many occasions that this *sutta* described detailed instructions for meditation practice in a systematic and sequential manner, guaranteeing results for the diligent practitioner - if not in seven days, in seven years.

In the previous Dhamma talks in this series we referred to the famous *Ānāpānasati sutta* (MN). This *sutta* described how to use of the breath, i.e. the awareness of the in-breath and the out-breath as the primary object of meditation. Similarly, in *suttas* such as the *Girimānanda sutta* (SN) and the *Kimbila sutta* (AN) the object of meditation described was the awareness of the contact of the breath. And the elemental manifestation discussed in this context was the air element (*vāyo phottabbha dhātu*).

The *Satipatthāna sutta* is an all-encompassing *sutta*, which begins with instructions to use the breath as the meditation object and devotes the entire first section towards this teaching. In the first *Kāyānupassanā* section the *Ānāpāna pabba* deals entirely with mindfulness of the breath. Thereafter, *Iriyāpatha pabba* is the segment that deals with 'bodily deportment', i.e. where the practitioner is invited to be fully aware of bodily postures –i.e. '*when walking he knows he is walking, when sitting he knows he is sitting, when standing he knows he is standing and when lying down he knows he is lying down*'. It is opening the door to *vipassanā* meditation practice.

Walking meditation requires a lot of effort on the part of the practitioner and can lead to rapidly understand deep aspects of the Dhamma. Such experiential realizations are more forthcoming during walking meditation than during the early stages of sitting meditation. These developments can motivate the practitioner to devote time for sitting meditation sessions. Thus, alternate walking and sitting meditation sessions galvanize one another and these give the yogi a very rewarding meditation experience. Such yogis realize the value of walking meditation, so much so that they make every endeavour to continue with it even at home. Moreover this practice helps a busy householder to continue with meditation practice even whilst fulfilling many responsibilities during a day, and particularly finding it hard to keep regular hours for sitting meditation.

The *Satipatthāna Sutta* is unique in that it takes the reader and practitioner step-wise, component by component, into developing mindfulness in all the bodily postures. After introducing and giving a detailed teaching on developing mindfulness on the breathing, in the next section the Buddha tells the *Bhikkhus* that he will teach another type of meditation, i.e. mindfulness of postures - *iriyāpatha bhāvanā*. The meditation practice on developing mindfulness of all four postures (i.e. sitting, standing, walking and lying down) is geared towards rapidly mastering the *vipassanā* practice.

> ..*Puna ca paraṃ, bhikkhave, bhikkhu gacchanto vā gacchāmī ti pajānāti*..

> '..when walking know that you are walking, when sitting know that you are sitting, knowing each posture thoroughly as a meditation exercise..'

A typical yogi or a *Bhikkhu* who is following the *Satipatthāna* practice will know every movement and every posture as and when he changes it. For instance, when going to the *dāna sāla*, he knows, '...*walking to the dāna sālā*', when going for a sitting: '..*going for a sitting meditation session*', and so on. The day-to-day activities that we all engage in can in fact be an excellent opportunity for meditation practice.

The classical portrait and visual image of a typical 'meditator' is one who is seated erect, cross-legged with eyes shut. Whereas the meditator who is placing mindfulness at every posture and during changes in posture, is similarly engaging in meditation practice.

Very often beginners to meditation are not aware of the importance of walking meditation. Moreover they are not aware of the beneficial effect that walking meditation will have on sitting meditation. Similarly there is little awareness on the value of walking meditation and the meditation on changing postures (*iriyāpata*), and the impact they will have on facing the challenges of day to day life.

Walking meditation requires a lot of effort on the part of the yogi. This is in sharp contrast to sitting meditation. *Vipassanā* practice (insight meditation) is effort based, i.e. effort and energy are pre-requisites for the development of *vipassanā* meditation and the eventual realization of *vipassanā* knowledge or insights. The teacher will notice that when the yogi practices walking meditation he/she progresses rapidly, and that meditation realizations are forthcoming in such a yogi. The energy mobilized during walking meditation is long-lasting and the yogi will come face to face with deep Dhamma understandings. This in turn will give extra momentum to practice sitting meditation and the sitting meditation sessions become more productive when preceded by walking meditation.

These personal experiences make the yogi accept and understand the value of walking meditation with conviction. With time, they learn how to integrate this practice into daily activity at work and at home. It's not easy for such practitioners to give up walking meditation in a hurry!

Sitting meditation classically develops *samādhi* or concentration, and facilitates the development of one-pointedness of the mind (*citta ekaggata*). *Samādhi* generated through sitting meditation is usually not very durable, particularly in the case of beginners. Regular practitioners of walking meditation find that walking meditation enhances the durability of *samādhi*. Usually in day-to-day life it's almost impossible to maintain a continuous state of *samādhi*. Whereas when yogis master walking meditation it becomes easier for them to maintain a state of *samādhi*, moment-to-moment, with mindfulness as a preceding factor.

When walking from one place to another, the yogi is advised to know that he is walking from A to B, and he is advised to note each step taken in that process. When contemplating step by step during that walking period he applies mindfulness during the entire walk. Such moment-to-moment mindfulness or awareness prevents the mind from becoming discursive and helps progress in the meditation practice. Such a yogi's mind will be with his body and will not be lingering in the past, or fantasizing about the future, or thinking of other persons or other events. Focused mindfulness on the body will energize the mind of the yogi. This is referred to as the development of *sampajañña - gocara sampajañña* or clear comprehension of purpose.

When a yogi has mastered this practice, he/she will rise from his sitting meditation posture with mindfulness established in the process of getting up, and will keep maintaining mindfulness while standing and during walking to his/her destination, thereafter.

When mindfulness thus placed on the body is not interrupted when changing from the sitting posture to standing and then walking, the yogi benefits much more than when mindfulness is confined to only the in/out-breath or to only rising/falling of the abdomen. Such a yogi's mindfulness develops versatility and thereby increases in durability.

Eventually the yogi will begin to experience when there is bodily movement and he/she will also experience an intention (or mental activity) governing that bodily movement. This experience is less forthcoming during a sitting meditation session, and particularly so for a beginner. This is because the posture remains stationary during meditation on the breath or on the abdomen, as opposed to when walking. During the latter, with increasing effort the yogi will be able to see the intention to move the leg and the accompanying movement - the former preceding the latter. There will be an understanding of cause and effect. During sitting meditation, with the attention only on one object, the tendency for *samādhi* is greater, and thereby the mind's precision and sharpness to penetratively discern the nature of the phenomena (mind and matter) may not be easily forthcoming.

Initially, in this manner the yogi practices walking meditation with mindfulness on the body. He knows when he intends to walk, and he knows when he is walking. He knows when he is about to turn and he knows when he is turning. He thus practices knowing each movement thoroughly, when walking. Indeed, walking can become a complete meditation practice for the yogi. He may contemplate knowing when he places the left leg and then the right leg, and when he/she repeats the same. The attention will now be on the two feet in sequence, left, right and then again left, right.

As the practice evolves the yogi could attempt to contemplate the walking step in three components: *lifting, moving, placing*. Whenever the yogi lefts the leg he may contemplate *'lifting'*, then *'moving'* and *'placing'*. This process needs sharper mindfulness and the yogi will notice many events occurring in the walking cycle. Initially this will be a challenge, but eventually as mindfulness improves it will become natural for the yogi to note the components in each step. Gradually he will know that the intention to lift the foot will precede the actual lifting and similarly, the respective intentions will precede moving and placing. This would make the yogi realize that an intention for every action always precedes each action. Gradually with practice, the belief that every action is just one compact unit will fade away as delusion becomes weakened. *Moha* (delusion) gets gradually replaced by clearer understanding.

If we observe the operation of an ordinary ceiling fan when it is switched on, we will see a fast rotating circle connected to the ceiling by a rod. We may even believe it is a single, rapidly moving circle. However, when we reduce the speed of the fan we will see that there are three blades attached to the rod and that is in turn attached to the ceiling, now rotating slowly. The three blades can be seen only when the speed of the fan is reduced. The 'compact unit' we saw, as a single circle is in fact a false belief. And when the electric supply is interrupted the blades won't rotate. Similarly, the feet move during walking only when an inner intention to walk is present. Without the 'mental command' the foot will not rise and move. But we will not see this when we walk without mindfulness. If walk slowly and mindfully, knowing each step as it rises, as it moves and as it is placed, then we will see this same process - each preceded by a mental command.

A yogi with sharpened mindfulness can discern that during walking, there is a series of bodily movements preceded by a series of intentions. With greater sharpness the yogi will discern that these series of movements appear and disappear on their own, independently. The mental activity or intentions too will appear and disappear independently. This is how mind and matter (*nāma-rūpa*) appear and disappear. With more practice the yogi will begin to see this quite naturally - the appearing and disappearing of intentions and bodily movements, during walking meditation. These are deep realizations that enable the yogi to get an understanding of Dhamma phenomena. *Pati vipassanā* is a term used to define this type of meditative realization, where the practitioner will use *vipassanā* practice to understand these realizations in one's own practice.

I remember at the start of my own meditation practice I didn't recognize the value of knowing clearly when engaging in a particular movement or about walking with contemplation. At the time when I had started practicing mindfulness I was a student and one day when walking on the road with my bag on one shoulder and some files in the hand, I suddenly remembered that I should start walking mindfully. On the middle of the road I began to contemplate – *'lifting the right leg and placing, lifting the leg and placing,..'*, and so on. I had to slow down the pace considerably in order to effectively contemplate in this manner. My colleagues who were walking with me had to go ahead since my pace had slowed down. For a while, with a lot of effort I was mechanically doing the contemplation but never realized anything. Then suddenly, I felt as though I was all alone and walking on the middle of the road. The contemplation on the steps I was taking had stopped and it had become an automatic/ 'robotic' movement. It was a strange experience of total contentment, and it was as though I was looking at myself whilst perched on top of a distant lamppost. But this experience lasted only a short while. Soon I had reverted back to the original situation of walking with the other pedestrians.

Once the diligent practitioner makes it a habit to contemplate every movement, (for example, *'walking to the door, opening the door, closing the door..'* etc) it becomes naturally ingrained in the mind. The practitioner begins to note every intention (*nāma dhamma*) during a preceding movement. After a while it comes very naturally, and the yogi's daily movements automatically slow down. Mindfully noting the intentions and the movements, gradually begin to occur as a normal practice. The more the yogi begins to experience the intention (*nāma*) and the corresponding movement (*rūpa*) as separate entities, the more the threat to the concept of a compact unit called 'self.' And the yogi will begin to observe him/herself from a distance as though observing another individual. This deep experiential realization of observing one's self as an outsider is referred to as *'parato'*. The experience of perceiving non-self (*anattā saññā*) is described in the following words: *anattato* (non-self), *suññato* (voidness), *ritthatho* (as a vacuum), *parato* (as an outsider), *thuccato* (as unworthy).

The realization of looking at one's self as if from outside does occur during sitting meditation, but it is more commonly experienced during walking meditation. If the yogi can consistently practice noting every intention and action when taking food, he will be able to watch taking the meal as if an outsider is watching. Moreover, the desire for food will lessen when mindfulness is steady and penetrative. Similarly our likes and dislikes towards different types of food, and opinions we have connected to food and drink will also lessen if we practice in this manner. This is not as easy as during walking meditation because during walking we are engaged in a neutral activity which doesn't generate desire. Eating a meal consisting of food of your choice on the other hand, will generate greed and desire!

Once the mind is firmly connected with the feet touching the ground, then it becomes a natural but monotonous movement.

The mind is then only with the movement of walking to and fro. In this situation it becomes easier to experience seeing one's self as if an outsider is watching.

During walking meditation, mastering the technique of watching one's self as if from outside (i.e. *paratō*) is the development of clear comprehension of purpose (*gocara sampajañña*). Having the realization that there is really no person/being that is walking, but that it is purely a series of phenomena (i.e. *dhammatha* - *nāma* and *rūpa*) arising and passing away, is a deeper understanding. Delusion becomes less and clear comprehension of the triple realities of impermanence, discontent and non-self (*asammōha sampajañña*) gets established. Sometimes it may be difficult for the pupil to communicate this understanding to the teacher. The pupil may even consider that such understandings are not relevant or important enough for reporting. Yet, a deep transformational impact is possibly taking place within the practitioner.

He/she may in fact lead his/her daily life as usual, whilst experiencing these changes but not giving any indication of such realizations to his associates. This is a significant milestone in the yogi's life where he practices the *satipatthāna* whilst realizing for himself the gradual evolution of his meditative journey.

For those who lead very busy lives in office or at home, walking meditation is a useful practice. It would function as a convenient bridge between the busy days and times when formal meditation is not possible, and the times available to devote exclusively to meditation. Particularly for practitioners of *vipassanā* meditation the value of this method of practice will be more relevant. In the case of tranquility (*samatha*) meditation practitioners, it will be less so. Because practitioners of *samatha* meditation suppress the five hindrances and consequently reach *samādhi* (one-pointedness) and rapidly reach a state where their posture is comfortably relaxed. They exert a lot of effort (*viriya*) to reach this state of *samādhi*. Therefore even though they have not practiced a lot of walking meditation, *viriya* is strengthened. Perhaps due to that reason, teachers of *samatha* meditation often don't emphasise the value of walking meditation.

Vipassanā practitioners develop momentary concentration (*khanikha samādhi*) in tandem with moment-to-moment awareness, and as a result maintain a continuous stream of *samādhi* irrespective of posture. This is referred to as *vipassanā samādhi*. Thus, in such yogis *samādhi* and *viriya* are balanced and continuous. Eventually he/she will be able to reach higher levels of *samādhi* during sitting meditation sessions even without devoting a lot of time for walking meditation before each sitting session. Initially, however, the yogi should devote equal times for walking and sitting meditation, in that sequential order. With increasing practice the skilled yogi will understand on his own, the methods to be adopted in order to balance these two important meditation practices. The yogi will also gradually realize experientially, the benefits of incorporating walking meditation into a daily meditation schedule in a systematic manner.

The Buddha demonstrated the value of this practice in many *suttas* and specifically referred to the *Caṅkamānisaāsa sutta* (AN – 111 29), a *sutta* exclusively devoted to this practice. Even though there may have been teachers, who were contemporaries of the Buddha, who would have practiced walking meditation in India at that time, their teachings had not been recorded and documented in relevant scriptures. Hence the paucity of available information on walking meditation by spiritual teachers, except for the Buddha.

Pancimé bhikkhave cankamé ānisansā? Katamé panca?

Bhikkhus there are five reasons for valuing walking meditation? Which five?

1. *Addhānakamatō hoti padāna kamatō* - When preparing for long journeys on foot, walking meditation helps because it gradually builds energy and prepares the person mentally and physically. The meditator organizes himself/herself and learns to spend the energy in stages and not all at once. During systematic walking meditation he/she develops great patience and builds the capacity for enduring the arduous task ahead. A person who multi-tasks and works in haste will not be able to last a long journey on foot. He will expend most of his energy at the beginning it self and will not have the ability to complete the many miles he had set forth to travel.

   Usually at the end of a rains retreat the Buddha undertook *cārika* (travelled long journeys on foot) for six to nine month periods. In preparation for these long journeys he would increase the daily practice of walking meditation. The latter would be a signal for his attendant Venerable Ānanda to know that a long journey was impending. Unlike today when famous monks would publicize their annual travel/teaching schedule well in advance, the Buddha never told anyone where he would be going, and when. Even his attendant would have to make a guess that the Master was preparing for a long journey.

2. *Satañ dhammaṁ na jaraṁ upeti* – A great deal of patience is cultivated when walking meditation is practiced diligently, if not, such a noble task like a long meditative journey cannot be completed successfully. Instead it will be interrupted mid-way. A regular walking meditator has enormous patience and endurance. The mind of such a person remains steady and undisturbed, and whatever impediments are faced he/she will manage them with dexterity. Similarly, whatever praise and gain he/she is showered with, will not neglect his/her own practice, i.e. he/she will not neglect the work of the internal *sāsana*. Such are the long-term spiritual benefits of walking meditation.

3. *Appābadhō hoti* – The body and mind, are equally balanced and free of stress. When walking meditation becomes an integral component of the yogi's daily practice, ailments and illness afflicting the body are less. Walking meditation is a balanced activity and it exercises both sides of the body equally. As we grow older and as we acquire more specific skills, the tendency for unequal

exercise for the body is greater. In childhood we uniformly exercise our entire body, since activity and play occupy the bulk of the day. This changes when aging takes place.

4. *Asitaṅ pitaṅ kāyikaṅ sammā parināmaṅgaccata* – Digestion of food and drink becomes easier. Ailments connected to the gastrointestinal system become less frequent. Soon after partaking food we feel lazy to engage in walking meditation and instead we prefer to sleep. If we had partaken just the correct amount of food we will not feel lazy and in fact we would feel energized to walk.

The ancient Sanskrit *slōka* (stanzas) mention how if after a very heavy meal we don't feel like even getting up, we will invariably have short lives. Similarly, if after a very heavy meal we climb trees, swim, run or exert ourselves excessively, again we will have short lives. But if we consume moderate amounts of food and engage in walking meditation thereafter, we will have long lives!

5. *Cankamādigatō samādhi cirattatikō hōti* – The quality of *samādhi* generated during walking meditation is more stable and long lasting. The *samādhi* generated after a 'successful' sitting meditation is difficult to protect after the sitting session is over. The moment we open our eyes and rise from the sitting posture, there is a tendency for the mind to become discursive when external impingements hit. Whereas the *samādhi* generated during walking meditation is generated then and there, amidst all external impingements, whilst the eyes are open and while we are

walking. Such a *samādhi* can be generated even after we leave the retreat centre and go home. When the yogi has mastered this ability he will be find that *samādhi* becomes reproducible and versatile. The *samādhi* will accompany the yogi where ever he/she goes – whether he is in a forest or resides in a royal palace!

I compare this to a situation where a patient is being nursed in an intensive care unit (ICU) and when he/she is subsequently taken to a general ward. In the former situation he/she is under constant supervision and medication, and is well protected. When he/she enters a general ward the susceptibility and exposure to multiple factors cannot guarantee the same care and protection as in an ICU.

In order to develop *samādhi* to such a degree in walking meditation, where it will have the qualities described above, the yogi needs to be consistent in practice and reach a stage where walking meditation becomes simply a process - mechanical, automatic and robotic, where the yogi will feel as if he/she is watching 'him/herself' walking from a far.

It now becomes clear why we advise yogis to practice walking meditation before a sitting session. The momentary concentration or *khanikha samādhi (or vipassanā samādhi)* generated during walking meditation will gather momentum speedily when the yogi commences a sitting meditation session, and thus *samādhi* will deepen. The Buddha's advice was: *'Come monk, dwell devoted to the practice of wakefulness. During day time, cleanse the mind of hindering qualities pacing up and down (caṅkamena) and sitting (nisajjāya)..'. Dhantābhumi Sutta 111.* The specific order of the two words the Buddha used, *(caṅkamena nisajjāya)* suggests clearly that pacing up and down should precede sitting.

However, you will note that the *Satipatthāna sutta* states in the *Iriyāpatha* Pabbam (Segment on Bodily Deportment) – *'gaccantōvā gaccāmītī pajānāti..'* (When walking a monk knows I am walking). The advice as appears in this *sutta* is to practice *ānāpānasati* first and then to practice walking meditation. Indeed some teachers do advise in that direction. My personal experience of having first practiced walking meditation before sitting meditation, and the benefits I accrued are what I am sharing with you all. Nissarana Vanaya was perhaps one of the original monasteries in Sri Lanka to pay attention to construct walking meditation paths, outdoor as well as indoors. Our ancient teachers emphasized the importance of this practice and its consequence.

I remember when Most Venerable Nānārāma Maha Thero was sick and warded in the ICU he would to ask us to remind him, when no one was nearby so that he could do a little walking meditation. Even when he was very ill he always did walking meditation for a brief period. He used to feel the immense benefit from that practice. That is why there are hand rails constructed alongside some walking paths at Nisarana Vanaya.

Therefore '*gaccantōvā gaccāmītī pajānāti*' needs to be understood in that context. Subsequently, the *sutta* states:

Ṭhito vā ṭhito'mhīti pajānāti,
Nisinno vā nissino'mhīti pajānāti
Sayānovā sayāno'mhīti pajānāti

(..when standing he knows I am standing, or when sitting he knows I am sitting, or when lying down he knows I am lying down..) In the *Karanīya metta sutta* it is described as;

Tittham caram nisinnanovā – Sayāno vā, yāvatassa
vigatamiddho Etam satim adhittheyya – Brahma metam,
vihāram idha māhu

(Whether he stand, walks, sits or lies down, as long as he is awake he should develop mindfulness in every posture. This is what the Buddha described as a Brahma life style, a life style of the highest conduct.)

image by MartinPettersson@flickr

After partaking alms, mindfully walking on the beach

'Come monk, dwell devoted to the practice of wakefulness. During daytime, cleanse the mind of hindering qualities pacing up and down (caṅkama) and sitting (nisajjāya). In the first watch of the night cleanse the mind of hindering qualities pacing up and down, and sitting. In the middle watch of the night go to sleep in the lion's posture reclining to the right side placing one foot on the other, mindful and fully aware, paying attention to the idea of waking up. In the last watch of the night, having got up cleanse the mind of hindering qualities, pacing up and down and sitting"

- ***Dantabhūmi Sutta MN 111***

Chapter Two

Instructions on walking meditation

The ideal walking path for walking meditation is an outdoor sandy path of about thirty feet in length and about two and a half feet in width. However during rainy seasons out door walking is not possible and therefore indoor walking paths will need to be utilized. Later in this book we will describe the methods to be used in preparation of outdoor and indoor walking paths.

Before commencing walking meditation the yogi should stand at one end of the path and note the posture of standing. He/she should spend a few moments contemplating on the standing posture. Standing, is one of the four postures recommended for a practitioner as described in the *Satipatthāna sutta*. The others are: sitting, walking and lying down. After the mind settles into the standing posture the yogi should then note mentally, that he is going to commence walking along the path in front of him. He could also reflect on the Buddha and all his disciples who used walking meditation as an integral component of meditation practice during ancient times, and how that practice has been handed down to us 2600 years later.

Thereafter the meditator should walk a few paces up and down the path in a relaxed manner. He/she should have his eyes directed about five feet in front of him, his hands clasped loosely either behind or in front of his body, and he should not glance around during these initial few minutes of relaxed walking along the path. This would enable the yogi to mobilize his body and generate energy, in readiness for the walking meditation that he/she will begin shortly. When the yogi reaches the end of the walking path he/she should slow down, and with complete mindfulness turn to the right and again note the standing position mindfully, re-direct his/her gaze to about five feet ahead and once again commence walking like he did before.

Initially the yogi should contemplate on the 'right foot' when he places the right foot in front and similarly the 'left foot' when he places the left. As the meditation gathers momentum the yogi will find that the mind is getting more and more directed on the body and the walking process that is underway. This practice of repetitive 'right foot', 'left foot' 'right foot', 'left foot', should be continued for close to an hour, relaxed and with no tension in the body. In this manner alternate sessions of walking and sitting meditation should be practiced on a daily basis, during a typical meditation retreat. Such a practice will increase the yogi's *sati* and will also help in generating *samādhi* during the sitting meditation sessions.

When practicing walking meditation in this manner, after about 20 minutes into the session, the yogi will be able to note each step as; *'lifting-placing'*, *'lifting-placing'*. This contemplation would apply to the right foot and the left foot in a sequential manner. The mind of the yogi becomes more and more trained to note the movement of the feet in this two-stage process of *'lifting-placing'*. Initially the yogi may know the difference between the left and the right foot, but subsequently he/she begins noting the differences in *'lifting-placing'*. The yogi should continue practicing in this manner until the mind becomes trained further in this particular practice of noting or labeling. As he/she progresses, the speed of walking will automatically slow down and the body will become more flexible and energized. With time, the yogi will understand that his/her capacity for this practice is increasing, and that he/she will be able to breakdown the process of each walking step into three: *'lifting-moving-placing'*. This indicates sharper mindfulness and the ability to note the process of walking more clearly than before. The mind of the yogi will be turning inwards with greater intensity.

On certain occasions some yogis may be able to break the step into six components: *'lifting-bending-moving-dropping-placing-pressing'*. This is a deeper contemplation with intensive mindfulness. However if during such a process the mind gets distracted the yogi may even lose his balance and fall. It is recommended that during walking meditation distractions should be avoided and even if someone speaks to the yogi, he shouldn't respond and should continue the practice. When external sense impingements such as sights, sounds, odours assail the yogi, he/should mentally note that the mind momentarily has left the walking process and that it has connected with the respective impingement, and thereafter that the mind has returned back to the walking. The yogi should try to keep mindfulness continuous, i.e. mindfulness is first with the walking, then it is with the sight/sound/odour, and then it is back with the walking. When these distractions occur the yogi shouldn't feel disheartened. In fact he/she has been provided with an opportunity to maintain uninterrupted mindfulness during different impingements. This cycle will be repeated during each walking meditation session. And the yogi gradually masters the art of maintaining uninterrupted and continuous mindfulness during every sense impingement that occurs during the walking session.

Distractions are particularly common at the end of the walking path, when the yogi is about to turn and make the return journey. Often the sense impingements (eg, a beautiful bird or a familiar sound) drag the mind away from the touch of the feet with the ground *(kāya prasāda)* to the sight *(cakkhu prasāda or sōta prasāda)* – and the mind, which was previously 'touching', has shifted to 'seeing' or 'hearing'. The sensory transaction and the relevant consciousness *(viññāna)* has thereby made a dramatic shift in this case body consciousness or *kāya viññāna* to eye consciousness or *cakkhu viññāna* or to ear consciousness or *sōta viññāna*. The yogi should simply know this shift of consciousness with mindfulness. He/she trains the mind to know each distraction as it occurs, and repeatedly brings the mind back to the object of meditation (in this case the feet touching the ground). This is to be done with no analysis, judgment or remorse. A trained mind will eventually master this ability so that whatever the external impingements occur at any sense door, the yogi will simply note it as *'seeing-seeing'*, *'hearing-hearing'* etc. and revert to knowing the walking.

Similarly, thoughts will invade the mind of the yogi during every session. The yogi should simply note the thought (as *'thinking-thinking'*) and immediately revert to walking. He/she should not analyze, fantasize or proliferate thoughts and memories when thoughts invade the mind. When thoughts invade the mind as they certainly will, the yogi should mindfully bring his/her attention back to the walking with a minimum time gap. This would further train the mind and enable the mind to deal with distractions efficiently with minimal loss of mindfulness. Knowing that the mind had strayed and returned, is a sign that the yogi's mindfulness has improved. And thereby the tendency to generate defilements has lessened.

There are occasions when yogis maybe advised by certain teachers to break the process of walking, into six stages, *'lifting-bending-moving-dropping-placing-pressing'*, however I would suggest that the three stage process of *'lifting-moving-placing'* alone would be adequate for the average practitioner.

Let us examine how mind and matter (*nāma rūpa*) operate during such an average walking meditation session.

Initially the intention to raise the leg operates in 'lifting' – this is *nāma dhamma*. When adverting the mind during the process *'lifting-moving-placing'*, intentions precede the action. And when the foot is placed on the ground *rūpa dhamma* (as the earth element - *pathavi dhātu*) is experienced. The movement of the foot is facilitated by the air element (*vāyo dhātu*). Therefore, as the yogi proceeds in this manner he/she will begin to note the way the *nāma-rūpa* operate, and how they arise and pass away with each step the yogi takes. With repetitive action the yogi's *sati, viriya* and *samādhi* develop gradually, and the mind becomes less discursive and more focused on the process of walking. Eventually he/she will generate effort so that noting of each step, the *nāma-rūpa*, and how they arise and pass away become natural and continuous. With increasing *Sammā Viriya* (Right Effort) the yogi may begin to understand cause and effect through walking meditation.

The yogi who has mastered the above sufficiently will have developed continuous *sati* and momentary concentration (*khanikha samādhi*) so that he/she would see all the minute details of the walking process clearly. What previously seemed like a compact unit of the foot touching the ground, may appear differently. The common example I cite is what appears as a long dark stick on a walking path, when looking closely, would turn out to be a string of black ants, hurriedly scurrying to and fro! A closer look would show the different features of each ant and how they differ from one another. A similar situation is when a movie picture is viewed on the silver screen. What we see as a continuous scene, is in fact composed of a series of individual frames, shown one after the other in rapid succession. Instead of knowing this reality we get engrossed by the continuously entertaining scenes and are deluded into experiencing either joy or sorrow. The reality is something totally different, and it is only a mind sharpened by mindfulness and concentration that can note this.

When the yogi has mastered this activity thoroughly he/she will be adopting three factors of the Noble Eight Fold Path, i.e. Right Effort, Right Mindfulness, Right Concentration (*Sammā Vāyāma, Sammā Sati and Sammā Samādhi*). Thus during walking meditation the yogi would be protected from already un-arisen defilements and due to lack of discursiveness, his/her mind would not be a fertile ground for already arisen defilements to proliferate. Thus fulfilling the four great efforts – *sathara sammappadāna viriya*. Such a mind would also be stress-free and would be developing capacity to deal with tension as and when it occurs. With time as walking meditation progresses, the yogi's intention and ability to advert the mind towards each step will improve steadily and he/she will have the determination to continue in the practice. *Sammā Sankappa and Sammā Ditthi* (Right Intention and Right View) gradually get established, thus fulfilling five factors of the Noble Eight Fold Path.

When the yogi progresses in this manner he/she will gradually find that the walking becomes automatic and 'robotic', monotonous and mechanical. He/she will begin to understand the entire walking meditation is only a process, and that it is simply an interplay of *nāma-rūpa*, and that there is no self/person/unit/entity behind the activity of walking. This is a powerful realization and is a prelude to the realization of non-self or *anattā*. Similarly when the process of walking becomes more and more a mechanical activity with full awareness, he/she would realize that all these arise and pass away. He/she will see impermanence in every step and movement, thus shattering the perception of permanence. This leads to the realization of impermanence – *aniccā*. The yogi will find that everything dissolves into nothing, everything he/she treasured with joy brings sorrow eventually, and thereby the perception of happiness/gladness (*subha saññā*) gets replaced by perception of sadness (*asubha saññā*).

In this manner with advancing practice the yogi will begin to see the connection between *nāma-rūpa* and cause and effect, during walking meditation. These realizations collectively will gradually deal a blow to one's conceit or *māna* (the feeling of 'I', 'me' and 'my-ness'). Consequently the view of 'myself' *diṭṭhi* and the attachment to what we traditionally refer to as 'mine' (*tanhā*) also get diminished gradually. *Tanhā, diṭṭhi* and *māna* are referred to as proliferative thoughts or *papañca dhamma* that perpetuate our long journey in *samsāra*. With gradual diminishing and eventual elimination of these deep-rooted defilements, the realization of the triple realities , i.e. impermanence, sorrow and non-self (*aniccā, dukkha and anattā*) becomes possible. Different yogis will experience these realizations differently, according to each ones past *kammic* heritage and practices.

Initially a yogi will find that developing and maintaining *sati* and *samādhi* in the manner described are difficult. But gradually with consistent practice and diligent effort he/she will master this efficiently. The direct benefit of mastering this practice is seen in day to day life. If *sati* is firmly placed on every movement and every posture *(iriyāpatha)* whatever we are engaged in, we have automatically reaped benefits. Whenever we face an adversity this practice comes in handy, because we have *sati* at the forefront, helping us to be in the present moment, thus reducing stress and tension. Eventually, with minimal effort we will be able to integrate this practice into daily life, to be in the present moment with full awareness, without judgment, analysis or remorse, irrespective of the situations we are faced with.

Uninterrupted and continuous mindfulness in all four postures is the ideal we should aim for. The power of mindfulness when developed enables this ability and the mind gets trained to note every intention and the action that follows it, and vice versa. For example: *'intention to sit and sitting'*, *'intention to stand and standing'*. After a while, it will feel as though the mind is 'training' us to note each intention and action. This is slow and gradual, but an extremely important juncture in the yogi's life. He/she will begin to note the changes occurring in the mind, and will be able to see intentions, feelings, emotions and thoughts as they arise and pass away. Thus from mindfulness of the body and postures *(kāyānupassanā)*, the yogi's path is paved to begin the next exercise in the *Satipatthāna sutta – Vedanānupassanā*.

Monk cleaning the walking path

Bhuktvā niṣīdatah sthaulyaṁ, tiṣṭhato balavardhanaṁ
Āyuṣcankramato nityaṁ, mṛtyur dhāvati dhāvatah

Vyāsakāra. 55.

'To one who sits after eating plumpness results, one who stands - grows in strength, one who walks has - longevity and to one who runs – Death is always close at the heels.'

Chapter Three

Preparation of the Walking Path (Promenade) or *Cańkamana*

Outdoor walking path

Just as much as we would choose a quiet environment for sitting meditation practice, we should similarly endeavor to choose a quiet place for walking meditation practice. An ideal walking path would be about 30-40 feet long and about three feet wide. Traditionally the walking path would have a slight elevation around it and a water trough around it as a moat, in order to prevent insects and reptiles from crawling onto the path. There would be a border or an access *(upacāra)* to the path about one-foot wide. This would be situated about four inches below the path.

The path would be flattened and covered with a layer of fine sand. The layer of sand would be slightly deep so that feet of the meditator would sink in just a little bit into the path. The surface should be soft and not firm to the touch of the soles of the feet. Grass, leaves, pebbles, stones or twigs should not be found on a sandy walking path. At the end of the walking path or promenade, there should be a fixed seat, which the meditator can use to sit if necessary. Some out-door walking paths may have a covering and a walled enclosure, for protection. Ancient Sri Lankan monasteries still have the ruins of such walking paths constructed according to traditional guidelines. An out-door walking path was always an integral part of temples, monasteries and spiritual places of worship. Ritigala, Mihintale, Anuradhapura are some places where such ruins can still be found. These ruins with remnants of walking paths bear testimony to how the inhabitants of such places of worship practiced walking meditation in those early years in Sri Lankan history. Unfortunately, in recent times walking paths are not a common feature in temples or monasteries.

Outdoor Walking Path: A cross section

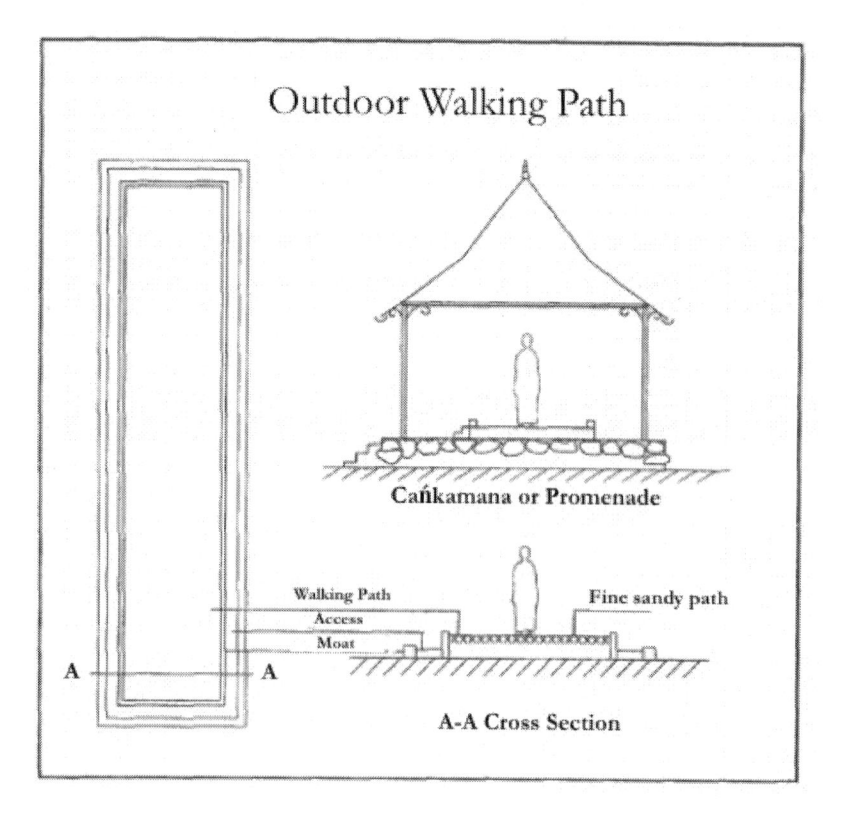

Outdoor Walking Path

Cañkamana or Promenade

Walking Path
Access
Moat
Fine sandy path

A-A Cross Section

I would advise that all meditators allocate a small area in their own garden or backyard, for the practice of walking meditation. These areas needn't have the ideal features of a traditional walking path described. They should be about 30 feet long, about two/three feet wide and have a line of bricks as its borders. It would very conducive if a layer of fine sand covers the walking path. I always encourage lay meditators to incorporate walking meditation into one's daily practice since it is a necessary component of the practice as we discussed earlier.

Nissarana Vanaya outdoor walking path with a fixed seat at the end of the path

Indoor walking path

These paths are situated inside the house and are protected from inclement weather. The designated area should be adequately ventilated and should not be used for any other purpose, other than for walking meditation. The length should ideally be 25-30 feet and the width about three feet. A chair placed at the end of the path is useful for the meditator to rest at the end of the walk. For aging meditators a handrail will be useful so that he/she can walk while holding on to the rail. There were times when a rope made of coir was fixed on the roof of the promenade (*ālambana rajju*) so that the meditator could hold on to the rope and pause for rest and then continue walking.

It is the practice at Nissarana Vanaya to use coir mats (*lanu peduru*) of 25-30 feet in length as walking paths. Coir mats have a rough surface and the meditator can experience different sensations on the soles when walking. These could be placed along lengthy corridors so that the meditator can use it for meditation once or twice a day. Walking on cement or on floor tiles is not advisable since these are hard surfaces and can have adverse effects.

Walking Meditation during a retreat at Nissarana Vanaya Indoor walking paths on coir mats (lanu peduru)

Monk in walking meditation at dawn

'One arouses an interest (candam janeti),
puts forth effort (vāyamati),
stirs up energy (viriyam ārabhati),
steadies one's mind (cittam pagganhāti) and
strives resolutely (padahati)
that pacing up and down paves the way to strenuous effort
which reaches its peak in the meditation seat.'

— *Upawāna sutta (SN)*

Chapter Four

Applying effort in Walking Meditation
From the Upawāna sutta (SN)

When describing the five Spiritual Faculties (*Indriya Dhamma*) and *Bala Dhamma* (both are components of the Thirty Seven Factors of Enlightenment or *Satthis Bodhipakkhiya Dhamma*), effort or *viriya* takes precedence over mindfulness or *sati*. In fact *viriya* is described in nine places in the Thirty Seven Factors of Enlightenment. However, when the *Bojjhanga Dhamma* (Enlightenment Factors) are discussed *sati* is described first and *viriya* is described later. Initially, in the early days of practice a lot of effort needs to be applied for a yogi to develop mindfulness. This is when *dhamma* are still young and are at *Indriya* and *Bala* levels of maturity, and these mental faculties have not yet reached the levels of development as seen in the *Bojjhanga Dhamma*. During those stages it is only with considerable effort and repeated contemplation that a yogi, when meditating, can bring the straying mind back to the object and re-establish *sati*. Therefore, although initially *viriya* facilitates and helps the development of *sati*, once *sati* is developed and matured to the level of *sati sambojjhanga, sati* in turn develops and reinforces *viriya* and keeps the mind awake and alert for the practice to continue. This is a natural evolution of the practice.

A novice meditator who applies initial effort *(āramba viriya/āraddha viriya)* will repeatedly contemplate on the object of meditation until he/she successfully comes face to face with the object. Just like in archery, initially the novice shooter will not directly hit the target. Eventually, with repeated practice he will hit the target, but first he/she will hit the target board in the periphery, and thereafter it is only after many attempts that he will hit the bulls-eye. Similarly a yogi will master the technique of using the appropriate amount of effort needed to develop mindfulness so that he will come face to face with the object of meditation.

Until then the meditator may have doubts about his/her ability to reach such a level mindfulness. Gradually the yogi develops courage and determination to repeat the exercise and eventually, after many attempts he/she will be able develop mindfulness in the present moment and be aware of everything that he/she does. Eventually however, the meditator will begin to feel monotony and even seem disinterested in the object of meditation. This is because after being used to staying with the object face-to-face; he/she will find that the object does not generate any excitement, fame or praise. In fact the boredom that ensues may even tempt the yogi to abandon the practice. At this stage a lot of extra effort and energy are needed by the yogi to take the practice forward. Although the yogi has actually evolved from the initial stage and is now at a more developed stage of mindfulness, he doesn't realize this and may even develop irritation towards the practice.

If a meditator recognizes this stage of monotony and boredom as a positive development, and decides to proceed forward in the practice, it is a welcome development but this is extremely rare. Such a yogi who will welcome monotony and understands its value would have developed mature *viriya* – i.e. *viriya* which is based on spiritual wisdom or *paññā*. This is referred to as *paggahita viriya* or *nikkhama dhātu viriya*. Such a yogi will seem to have more disturbances during meditation when reaching this stage of the practice. The mind is clearer and more sensitive now, and the yogi will be aware of the invasion of thoughts, the mind's incessant thought-flow and inner-chatter very clearly. Similarly, aches and pains are also prominent. Some yogis may feel as though he/she has lost *sati* and *samādhi* and may feel disappointed and frustrated. He/she may even consider abandoning the practice. The yogi who feels the urgency for spiritual liberation (*saṁvega*) will know that if he/she leaves the practice at this stage, they will once again return to the domain of the external sense pleasures due to greed (*tanhā*), and consequently will keep generating more defilements. When exposed to the world of the six senses, the aches and pains, and monotony will disappear, albeit temporarily. However a yogi with a genuine sense of urgency will bear up these discomforts and will continue to stay with the practice.

The meditation master is critical at this stage, so that he can advise the yogi to keep practicing despite all the hardships. Such a yogi will not abandon the practice and succumb to sensual temptations which mask these hardships, and prevent the realization of the truth, thus foregoing seeing things as they really are. The yogi, whose *viriya* has developed and is supported by *paññā*, reminds him/herself that the Buddha and all his disciples traveled this same path and realized the Noble Truth of Suffering in an identical manner. This recollection will inspire him/her and will energize him/her to strive diligently.

Every moment we are not in *sati/appamāda*, we are heedless (*pamāda*) and we will keep collecting *kilesa* or defilements. When we are in *sati* and when we are aware of every present moment we are in, we will experience the discomfort of previously, existing defilements. We also know that during every new thought-moment (*cittakhana*) that arises, we are fully aware of the state we are in, and that we don't generate new defilements. Therefore when in *sati,* un-arisen defilements don't arise during the new thought-moments.
 The yogi is simply aware of the existing pains and discomfort, and he/she bears these with fortitude due to an advanced state of *viriya*: *nikkhamadātu viriya*. Moreover, the yogi knows that it is only during these difficult moments that existing defilements get extinguished. Offering *pūja, dāna* or observing *sīla* doesn't help us to annihilate *kilesa*. Only being in *sati,* moment-to-moment, does so. This is a very difficult stage to tolerate and transcend, and the modern generation is not equipped to do so. Exposure to newer technologies and scientific advancements, and the multitude of distractions that have come in their wake, have gradually eroded the coping skills of the new generation. Similarly fear and shame have

lost their importance. In such a milieu it is difficult to develop these noble traits as exposed to us by the Buddha.

The Buddha extolled the virtues of walking meditation in the context of developing such durable and advanced *viriya*. He said that walking meditation enables the development of strong *viriya* which strengthens the yogi's resolve to undertake a very long meditative journey. Such a yogi will invariably take the journey right up to the end, i.e. to *nibbāna*.

Walking meditation is highly recommended by the Buddha after a meal, so that digestion becomes easy and sloth and torpor, and indolence get reduced. Similarly walking meditation helps the alleviation of many illnesses. It also helps older people who like to commence meditation practice for the first time. Parents, who may like to introduce the practice of meditation to their children, should begin this introduction with walking meditation. I always advise meditators to construct a simple walking meditation path in their own back yard or garden, so that it becomes easy to integrate the practice into the daily schedule. I ask yogis to keep trying out this practice repeatedly, bearing up the monotony that ensues at a particular stage. I have heard how some yogis adopt various techniques to keep the practice going- eg, some even walk backwards on the sandy path to keep mindfulness steady and continuous. Some may even walk on a wall. Can we ever walk backwards on the walking path unless mindfulness is strong? Similarly, can we walk on a wall unless we are exceptionally mindful? All these techniques which will bolster the yogi's keenness to pursue walking meditation, are commendable.

Walking meditation practice was very common in ancient Sri Lanka, but its appeal had diminished with time. My wish is that this practice is rejuvenated and that it once again occupies the important position it did in a meditator's life. Similarly, we should learn to use the practice of walking meditation in our daily lives. For instance, when walking short distances from the bus stop to a destination or from our home to the corner store. Try avoiding using vehicles, and engage in walking mindfully during such short journeys. The benefits you will reap will be enormous. The contact of the soles of feet with the earth will gradually aid the development of *viriya*.

The Buddha walked miles and miles across the northern part of India without any foot ware, i.e. *cārika*. So did his disciples. Today, *cārika* is practiced by few exceptional monks only. If we renew the walking practice and bring back the promenade to its rightful place we can revive a lost but valuable art of meditation.

The Buddha said that during walking meditation if at a particular stage, the walking becomes 'automatic' or 'mechanical' – can we still watch that situation as if from outside and continue the practice? When thoughts invade the meditators mind, can we still keep walking as if we are walking on a carpet of thoughts with minimal effort? Sights and sounds assail the meditator from every angle, yet can he/she notice the foot touching the ground - the rough edges of the sand scraping the skin of the feet, the contours of the soles of the feet as they move on the sandy path, step by step, to and fro? Indeed, this is an ideal situation where the yogi's mindfulness is placed on the soles of his/her feet despite any disturbance. When this practice evolves the yogi will be developing *sati and samādhi* in tandem, and they will be steady and durable.

S*amādhi,* which we develop painstakingly during a sitting meditation session, could leave us no sooner we rise from the session. This does not happen in the case of walking meditation because the *samādhi* developed through this practice is generated whilst the body is fully active and walking with intention, and with the eyes open. Furthermore *samādhi* is reinforced while the yogi makes a turn, at the end of the promenade, and hence its strength and durability. The yogi who commences a sitting meditation session soon after walking meditation will find that the mind settles almost instantly, and that *sati* and *samādhi* gets established soon. This is similar to an athlete who warms up before the event, and fares better on the track than the one who hasn't. Walking meditation is a warm-up in preparation for a sitting.

However, a beginner will not be able to realize the value of this practice. It is only after many trials and errors that he/she will perfect the art. Usually a beginner with a novice's mind will feel remorse that *sati* and *samādhi* aren't settling in with ease. It is only after walking meditation is mastered to a degree, that the yogi will understand how it will benefit the sitting session.

Unfortunately today, it is not often that meditation teachers and meditation centres place a lot of emphasis on walking meditation. In fact the active practice of yogis in a meditation centre can be gauged by the manner in which the promenades are used. It is also rare to find attention being paid to constructing walking paths in certain meditation centres. This is unfortunate and it is a testimony to the scant respect paid to the practice of *caṅkama*. If we visit ancient sites of worship in cities like Anuradhapura and we see walking meditation paths, I could guess these were used by revered *bhikkhu*s and nuns, and perhaps some of them were *arahants*. Even if we see beautiful temples and shrines with ornate statues of the Buddha and his disciples, we could have doubts if the occupants of the temples had actually practiced walking meditation as prescribed by the Master himself. Ornaments, decorative pujas and ritualistic paraphernalia don't in fact belong to the Buddha's teachings. Walking meditation does. This teaching cannot be attributed to any other faith but Buddhism, since no other spiritual teacher or contemporary of the Buddha taught this practice. The Buddha was the classic teacher, the advocate and practitioner of this method of meditation – he, in fact 'walked the talk'.

I feel happy when I see modern houses where a separate space has been allocated for walking meditation. The inhabitants of these houses are true practitioners and followers of the Buddha's teachings. At Nissarana Vanaya we place lot of emphasis on walking meditation. This is because it builds *viriya* and determination to overcome all obstacles, and it is the perfect antidote for sloth and torpor, and laziness. Pains, sounds and thoughts – the commonest impediments to a sitting meditation session, will be present during walking meditation as well. But these are easily overcome. Pains get less since we are active and energetic while on the promenade. Sounds (and sights, smells) assail us, but we have a coarse primary object in the form of the feet touching the ground to focus on (as opposed to the refined in/out-breath during a sitting), and therefore sounds fade into the background. Thoughts come and go, and after a while when *sati* and *viriya* have been mobilized to *nikkhama dhātu* level, we would feel as though we are walking on a carpet of thoughts! The soles of the feet would be walking on a series of thoughts and we remain unaffected. For the first time we may realize that these intruding thoughts don't belong to 'me', 'myself' or 'I'. Such a yogi would find that the sitting meditation session, which immediately follows walking, is far more successful. He/she would realize that despite pains, thoughts and sounds the attention on the breath could be maintained, better than before.

When continuing in this manner the yogi would find that observing the breath becomes easier and continuous. Gradually he/she would note the beginning, middle and end of each breath, and subsequently he/she will note the elemental nature of the breath and advert the mind to the elements – *dhātu manasikāra*. As he/she goes deeper into the practice, sounds may recede insignificantly into the background and series of thoughts may just come and go with minimal impact.

Similarly, pains may not be felt even though severe. These indicate progress in meditation.

Walking meditation is a balanced exercise during which the entire body is active. Similar to swimming, climbing a coconut tree and horse riding, walking meditation exercises the entire body. A yogi once mentioned that he feels as though a person is slowly walking whilst waist-deep in water, where the entire arc the foot takes, moving against the resistance of the water, can be felt distinctly. Some yogis say they feel as though a bicycle is being peddled in slow motion. All the bones in our feet and ankles are intricately placed, and they work in synchrony and in perfection to make these delicate movements. A mature yogi, after much experience will know the way the joints in the feet move with each step. He/she will reach a stage when every movement of the feet, whether he/she is lifting the foot in front or placing it behind or turning, is clearly known and perceived – *'pacchāpuré saññī*.

Venerable Kaṭukurunde Ñānānanda, in his book (*Walk to Nibbāna*) refers to the advice the Buddha gave Venerable Mahā Moggallāna when he found the latter feeling drowsy during meditation. The Buddha offered seven 'waking pills' to Venerable Moggallāna and said, when 'administering the seventh pill':

If drowsiness does not leave you when you are dwelling this way, then Moggallāna determine the pacing up and down, caṅkamana, being conscious of the behind and the before 'pacchāpuré saññī with sense faculties turned inwards and with mind un-strayed'. (Pacalāyana Sutta – AN 1V)

Eventually, even during day to day work the yogi will master the ability to know clearly, every posture change and to know that all our movements are simply processes.

It is said the Buddha had feet where the soles would make perfect contact with the earth, as though they stuck/clung to the earth–*supatitthitha pāda*. One meditation master described this in the following way, saying: *'Walk as if you are kissing the earth with your feet'*. At the beginning we need to gently walk on the promenade with no extra effort and be totally aware of the movement of walking. This is more than adequate at the start. With time and with natural evolution of the practice, realizations will come to the yogi. Until then, my advice is to allow this process to evolve with minimal intervention. With time, the yogi will be surprised at the experiences he/she will face first hand.

I often compare this to how, when Prince Siddharta placed his feet on the ground for the first time, each step is said to have resulted in a blooming lotus. Such would be how realizations would bloom each time the feet touches the ground with complete mindfulness and steadfast *viriya*. The mind of the yogi is free from defilements generated from the six senses during this period (i.e. *suvimuttam me cittam)*. There is perfect equilibrium during the walk on the promenade and the yogi is steady and will not sway to a side, when the mind is pure and *kilesa-free.*

Even though sights, sounds, thoughts or smells would assail the yogi, he/she is walking as though on auto-pilot and is unaffected by these impingements. There is a contentment that is to be experienced when he/she is free from the sense pleasures. This is where primordial energies are fully active and the yogi is free of defilements. The yogi who is spiritually mature and has had sufficient exposure to the teachings of the Buddha will know the value of this stage of the practice. It's a very fulfilling stage where greed, conceit and views (*tanhā, māna, ditthi*) are held at bay and only primordial energies are present. The Buddha advised the meditator to treasure this stage and regard it as spiritual seclusion with contentment.

According to Abhidhamma scriptures and the Commentaries, the *passa panchamaka dhamma* describe five mental factors that operate in our minds. i.e. *phassa, vedanā, saññā, cetanā, manasikāra*. Accordingly, the generation of defilements begins with *phassa (*contact) and it is only thereafter that *vedanā* take place (where we experience feelings) and thereafter *vitakkha and vicāra* – initial and applied thought formation. These are followed by proliferation of thoughts. However, Venerable Sāriputta describes the mental factors in the *Sammā Ditthi sutta* in this order: *vedanā, saññā, cetanā, phassa, manasikāra*. He said that before contact with the object (i.e. before *phassa)*, we have feelings and memories about that object and that it is due to these that a relevant *cetanā* brings us into contact with the object. Hence, *cetanā* precedes *phassa*. We are surrounded by impingements on all six senses but we make contact with only one object per given moment. This means there is a filtering process and a selection. This selection is based on memories and feelings, which are in turn dependent on one's inherent pre-dilections and pre-dispositions. All of these create an intention, a *cetanā* and this precedes *phassa*.

A yogi will never be able to see this sequential activity of how mental factors (*nāma dhamma*) operate, before contact occurs, even with substantial training. We can only experience this situation during meditation after *phassa* has taken place. We can never realize experientially how a particular object was chosen by the mind. Only the Buddha could see how contact with an object is pre-determined.

During the past twenty years or so this subject has been discussed by meditation masters: *'how does the mind get dragged to make contact with one particular object when so many objects are assailing the six senses of the yogi?'*

'Which mental factor is responsible for adverting the mind towards one particular object, with which it will make contact?' (Reference: Dasuttara Sutta Part 11, Dhamma Talks - www.damsara.org)

Manosancetanā or manosankhāra is the mental factor that adverts the mind in the manner described. *Manosancetanā* are mental factors which reside in the deep recesses of the mind and we cannot usually see how they operate. Only during deep meditation when *kāyasankhāra* have subsided and after deep *samādhi* has set in, can an experienced yogi see how they operate.

During walking meditation, when the mind is dragged towards a visual image, can we discern which *Manosancetanā* prompted this shift of mind – from the foot/ground to the visual image? Will we be able to see the mechanism of this operation? The only way to understand this process is to allow the situation to repeat it self, over and over again, the next day and the next. Keep allowing the mind to get dragged away and watch what happens.

Gradually the yogi will understand that when the mind is on the foot touching the ground, it is *kilesa*-free i.e, the mind is occupying an oasis and it is in a safety-zone. When it jumps to a sight or a sound, it has entered a dangerous-zone or a defilement-zone; one which generates *tanhā, māna, diṭṭhi,* the defilements that perpetuate *samsāra*. Again the mind will revert to the foot and to the touch of the ground, the safety-zone. But the cycle will repeat itself. For a yogi who is engaged in walking meditation in the midst of a multitude of objects and challenges, to be able to see this shift of mind occurring at lightning speed, milli-second to milli-second, and to watch the process with a balanced mind, needs a lot of practice, determination and unwavering, steadfast mindfulness. In fact the yogi would have reached the meditation stage of *Dhammānupassanā* (Ref: S*atipaṭṭhāna sutta)* in his/her practice.

Such a yogi, with time, will clearly know how the mind flits from the danger-zone to the safety-zone, repeatedly. He will master the ability to remain equipoised during these mind-moments *(cittakkhana)* – *akālika* - events, and will know that his/her *saddhā, sīla and sati* are intact. This skillful understanding is a reflection on the yogis spiritual maturity and the developing *paññā*. If not, and if ignorance and delusion (*avijjā*) prevail, when the mind moves from the foot to an external object there will be remorse and generation of defilements. An unprepared meditator will generate irritation and remorse when the mind jumps. The Buddha advocates non-remorse, non-irritation and acceptance of any eventuality with equanimity. Therefore the meditator should go fully prepared and equipped with the teachings of the Buddha, so that he/she will understand these meditative experiences with wisdom.

With advanced *viriya (paggahita viriya)* the yogi begins to sporadically experience a stage of fulfilling contentment. . He/she may experience this when seated and is fully aware of the posture. Similarly when lying down or standing. Words cannot completely describe this experience of being free of defilements and in full contentment. Naming or identifying this experience becomes difficult. Relatively or comparatively, a yogi who is sitting down may be able to say: '*I know I am not standing*'. *Sati* will also be well developed when this stage of *viriya* is experienced. The inability to name/label an impingement or experience would mean that the mind is getting pure gradually and that it is free from defilements. Experiencing primordial energies as monotony or boredom is the ideal situation to be in.

When *sati* evolves from *āramma dhātu* to *nikkhama dhātu* to *parakkama dhātu*, the yogi experiences sensations as and when they occur, and this indicates that *sati* has evolved to an extent that even if one asks it to leave, *sati* will not leave!

Maha Si Sayadaw used to say that whenever a severe pain is experienced, a seasoned meditator maybe at the threshold of a *vipassanā* insight. If the yogi abruptly interrupts the session of meditation due to pain he may lose that valuable realization. Whereas if he stays with the practice whilst bearing up the pain, growth of *viriya* is happening gradually during these process and this evolution happens internally. *Viriya* is not visible to an external observer as an exhausting effort by the yogi.

When the yogi's endurance grows and the meditation progresses despite discomfort, pain or boredom, he/she will experience mild rapture (*pramōda or* immature *pīti*) because he/she knows that defilements are kept at bay during these stages of meditation. This manifests internally as joy. This stage is also a prelude to developing mature *sati sampajañña*. Eventually these stages will result in fully-fledged *pīti*.

The Buddha said that when a meditator experiences severe pain and serious illness, that would be the time he will experience *nibbāna*. When severe pain assails, if the yogi becomes fully aware of its nature and severity and stays with the pain, it would be easy for him/her to transcend the pain. No amount of medication will give that deep experience. In fact it is said that experiencing *nibbāna* and transcending severe pain occur almost simultaneously. Being completely and fully aware of the pain when present, will herald significant realizations. *Paripunna viriya, i.e viriya* that is capable of enabling the yogi to bear up serious pain with complete mindfulness, is a critical milestone in a yogi's life. In fact we need to welcome pain and disturbances during meditation. And if *saddhā* and *sati* remain uninterrupted in the face of pain and disturbances, we would have reached an important stage in our practice.

Therefore endurance and fortitude are essential to allow the meditation practice to mature. This is when *viriya sambojjhanga* begins to emerge and shine a powerful light on our practice.

'image credits to http://www.tathagata.org/'

Ovādacariya Sayādaw U Paṇḍitābhivaṃsa In walking meditation with the aid of a walking stick accompanied by two monks

Sayadaw U Panditha - Bhivamsa answering questions

Is walking meditation helpful in daily life?
Yes. A short period—say ten minutes of formal walking meditation before sitting—serves to focus the mind. Also, the awareness developed in walking meditation is useful to all of us as we move our bodies from place to place in the course of a normal day.

What mental qualities are developed by walking meditation?
Walking meditation develops balance and accuracy of awareness as well as durability of concentration.

Can one observe profound aspects of the Dhamma [dharma] while walking?
One can observe very profound aspects of the Dhamma while walking, and even get enlightened!

If you don't do walking meditation before sitting, is there any disadvantage?
A yogi who does not do walking meditation before sitting is like a car with a rundown battery. He or she will have a difficult time starting the engine of mindfulness when sitting.

When walking rapidly, what should we note? Where should we place our awareness?
If you are moving fairly rapidly, make a mental note of the movement of the legs, "Left, right, left, right," and use your awareness to follow the actual sensations throughout the leg area.

Should you watch your feet?
Do not watch your feet unless this becomes necessary due to some obstacle on the ground; it is unhelpful to hold the image of a foot in your mind while you are trying to be aware of sensations. You want to focus on the sensations themselves, and these are not visual.

What can people discover when they focus on the sensations of walking?
For many people it is a fascinating discovery when they are able to have a pure, bare perception of physical objects such as lightness, tingling, cold and warmth.

- http://www.lionsroar.com/how-to-practice-vipassana-insight-meditation/

Chapter Five

Questions & Answers on Walking Meditation

1. *During walking meditation the coarseness experienced on the soles of the feet is as though the feet get drawn towards the ground. I feel some discomfort when placing the foot but then feel comfort when the foot is raised. Can you please explain how the mental factors (cetasika) operate during this process? And should we simply contemplate the left and right feet as and when they are raised and* **placed?**

Try your best to allow the process to occur naturally without contemplation or facilitation. Be mindful of the materiality (*rūpa dhamma*) – hardness, softness, lightness when placing and raising the feet, but don't try to pre-empt or contemplate mentality (*nāma dhamma*). Don't try to investigate and analyze what is going on during the walking meditation process. However, if certain experiences or realizations occur naturally, don't try to reject those as well. During walking meditation we focus on *kāyānupassanā* (knowing the body in the body) and we don't try to understand the mind, i.e. *cittānupassanā*. If we engage in the latter we may sacrifice the simplicity of the meditation practice as prescribed by the Buddha. We run the risk of allowing deductive knowledge/inferential knowledge to creep in and we may miss out on the experiential aspect, and we may even regress in our meditative practice.

We need to remember that in walking meditation we intentionally (i.e. with a *cetanā*) place mindfulness on the process of walking whilst contemplating the right/left feet, whereas in sitting meditation without any intention (with no *cetan*ā) we allow the breath to manifest naturally and then mindfully observe the in/out-breath. Both these types of meditation and the diversity of mindfulness are important. Moreover, in day to day work and whilst multi-tasking, the experience derived during walking meditation helps when trying to place mindfulness on each of our activities. Therefore during a meditation retreat we practice mindfulness during non-intentional activity (sitting meditation), during intentional activity (walking meditation) and a variety of other activities. The latter two don't result in deep *samādhi* as opposed to during a sitting session, but nevertheless are of great value when developing the practice of mindfulness.

2. During walking meditation I find that the sensitivity of the left sole differs from the right. This experience is quite significant irrespective of the nature of the walking meditation path (e.g. sand, carpet, grass, cement floor). I also note very strange experiences like feeling as though I am falling into a pit and as though I am walking outside the path. These experiences make my mindfulness suffer.

This is natural. Some of us have different sensitivities in the different feet/soles; similarly this experience can be forthcoming in relation to our palms. But this is a meditation experience. Don't try to investigate this proactively. This indicates that the practitioner is beginning to discover traits in relation to his body.

When mindfulness has become established during sitting or walking, it is not uncommon to experience bizarre manifestations as described. When the meditation object and the mind become closely aligned to each other, after a while certain changes occur. This is because the mind is not used to experiencing such uniformity. The mind's nature is to roam around, flitting from one object to another looking for variety. Alignment with only one object for a long time is not conducive to the conventional mind and it is as though the mind has undergone a paradigm shift. Hence these manifestations. The same thing can happen if we decide to slow down our usual activities and work at a slower pace than what we are used to.

I consider this as an indication of good progress in meditation.

3. Although at the beginning walking meditation is very pleasant I find that after a while boredom and monotony sets in.

Always be well prepared when commencing walking meditation, because monotony is inevitable after a while. Please remember that being with monotony and boredom is an indication of getting close to *nibbāna* whereas getting distracted with sensory pleasures would mean perpetuation of *samsāra*.

We need to test ourselves and see if our personality is strong enough to withstand boredom and to swim against the tide. The ability to tolerate *nibbidhā* (disenchantment) is a feature of a yogi who is developing capacity to reach *nibbāna*. However, if disenchantment is based on irritation or anger then it is very negative and won't direct us towards *nibbāna*. Instead, the aim should be to cope well with insipidity/boredom and to keep meditating (during walking/sitting, daily life) despite the disenchantment. *Tapas* – austerity, meaning such a restrained conduct which is conducive to mental training, adopted by spiritual persons.

I am not advocating that you proactively seek discomfort and austere living. That would be tantamount to a*tthakilamathānuyoga* – which the Buddha did not advocate.

4. Is it advisable to do walking meditation for a few minutes at the beginning with the eyes closed? I find that this helps me.

This is good because it indicates that the yogi is now experimenting with various ways of engaging in the practice. The mind is being challenged to deviate from tradition and to accommodate non-conventional modes of practice. This is referred to as neurobics where new circuits in the brain open up and start functioning – the brain is getting trained! In fact I would encourage to try further methods of practice, such as doing walking meditation while walking backwards, or while being on a wall or even trying to do walking meditation while walking backwards on a wall!

The novice however, is advised to not close the eyes when doing walking meditation. After the practitioner gains experience and gets familiar with the walking path he may try these additional methods. Scientific research shows that various techniques and skills can be used to stop the brain from ageing. That helps our brains to remain alert, agile and 'awakened' even while we are growing old.

If not our brains will remain inside the same rut and we will go on with no 'awakening' of the brain.
Mindfulness plays a big role in these initiatives and helps the brain to get re-wired and energized.

5. Can you explain how walking meditation can be practiced as six stages?

The Venerable Maha Si Sayadaw technique advises that walking meditation be contemplated in six stages. But this method can be a little complicated at the start. And therefore yogis are advised to start with three stages –initially as left, right; thereafter as lifting, placing and subsequently noting the feet as lifting, moving, placing (i.e. three stages). Please refer the Visuddhimagga for further details.

6. When engaged in walking meditation slowly I feel sleepy. If I increase the speed and then follow it with a sitting I find that helpful.

My advise regards the speed of walking meditation is to try it out and see which works best for you. Sometimes slowing down may become artificial and not help the yogi. I always ask yogis to initially use the speed that comes naturally. Don't introduce artificial speeds in to the pattern that suits you most. Different yogis may find that the speeds they are individually used to, differ from one another. The body will determine what's best for you. Sloth and torpor often get reduced when increasing the speed. Always challenge the mind and try various methods to overcome these hindrances. Our mind will always throw up excuses, hindrances, crafty ideas to encourage us to stop the practice. We should be even craftier and not allow the mind to have its own way. If the mind ambushes us lets work out a counter-ambush, a guerilla ambush!

When engaged in *ariyapariyeshana* (the Noble Quest) this is to be expected. In the *Chūlasihanāda* sutta the Buddha describes the variety of measures he had to adopt to overcome the tricks and traps of the mind during the six years period of austerities the Bodhisatva spent, prior to reaching enlightenment.

7. During walking meditation I notice both feet and the steps I take, whilst at the same time I note the thoughts that come and go. In fact even when normally walking (when not in meditation) I have the same experience. Are these two situations any different from one another?

In fact we can take this question and describe it as three scenarios:
− During walking meditation every detail of each step can be noticed with clarity. The individual characteristics of each step can be observed in detail
− When in walking meditation knowing the walking process whilst noting sounds, thoughts and sights that come and go
− In day to day life we note our walking in a similar fashion and also simultaneously note how thoughts come and go

Viññāna tricks us to make us see these as three distinct entities, and makes us question the veracity of each experience and makes us choose one from another! When in fact it is the same situation experienced in three different ways. *Viññāna* tries to exploit every situation in an extremely fraudulent and deceptive manner, so that doubts arise in our minds and we resort to proliferation of thought - *papañca*. We may think we have an inquiring mind and that our intellectual curiosity is at a height. In fact this is not so. We are simply succumbing and becoming victims of the traditional tricks of *viññāna*.

Can we proceed with the practice without creating doubts in our minds and can we accept things as they arise with no questioning or analysis? This is a significant deviation from what we have been trained to do – academically and professionally. We may then seem like not having a strong personality. But that's the only way to not succumb to the traps laid out for us. The Buddha warns us that each time we begin to question and doubt situations, we have left the present moment. We have started riding our thoughts. We have begun the journey of *papañca* and question the Dhamma the teaching, and wondering if this is included in the Abhidhamma, Vinaya pitaka and much more. In fact we have become the victims and the *viññāna* has become the king!

That is indeed the task and the work assigned to *viññāna* – to perpetuate doubt and create situations where worry and restlessness ensue, i.e. to stir the pot! It is the most difficult of the five aggregates to identify and isolate. It is much sharper and shrewder than you will ever know. Therefore my advice is to not leave room for *viññāna* to take the upper hand, to create conflict in our minds and thereby fertilize the 'I, Myself, Mine' factor and thus perpetuate *kilesa*. Whenever divisions are created and choosing/judgments take place only the 'I, myself, mine' factor wins.

My advice is to remain uninvolved and unperturbed whatever issue comes your way. This is not traditional meditation, but application of deductive knowledge, *yoniso manasikāra* and correcting one's view. This is a mastery of one's mind to approach issues with wise reflection. This is the approach to wisdom.

Main thing is not to worry and Mind Your Own Business!

8. ***During walking meditation I can proceed smoothly with no contemplation and with minimum thoughts. I also feel quite equanimous. Do you have any advice to offer to further progress on this path?***

My advice is to continue this repeatedly. There may be times that walking meditation proceeds very smoothly. Yet there may be times when thoughts and other disturbances occur. But if you can develop resilience to proceed with the practice with a balanced mind despite obstacles, then you have progressed. The ideal situation would be for the walking meditation to be almost 'robotic' or a mechanized process where you are simply a passive observer. This situation leads to a direct taming of *kilesa*. You need to replicate the same during day to day life. Then such work is done with no stress and you will feel fresh at the end of the day and may not need any rest! You will soon realize that this 'freshness' and lack of stress is not due to external factors or due to the posture you adopt. It is simply how the mind is getting adjusted to disturbances and still is able to remain balanced.

9. *I have noticed that over the time I am able to sit longer during sitting meditation and that despite external disturbances I can maintain my meditation. This is the same for walking meditation.*

This is good, but eventually you will note that the meditation will not be limited to postures and that even when you finish a sitting, mindfulness will not leave you. And despite disturbances you will be able to continue having *sati* at the fore-front. During day to day work, *sati* will always be with you from waking up until going to sleep. Then you have matured in the practice. The duration of the sitting and postures become irrelevant, and meditation with *sati* at the helm proceeds independent of such situations.

10. *During an hour and half of walking meditation, towards the latter stages I noted the sensations felt at the soles of my feet very clearly. In addition I felt tingling sensations on my face. I did not feel any discomfort. Even after an hour and a half, I only felt good and realized that the mind was at ease when it was doing only one thing with full awareness. Is this comfortable feeling due to the fact the mind was not racing to the past and excited by the future?*

Only simple and straightforward things give pleasantness. Anything that is curved/convoluted or complicated will not generate pleasantness. A straight line is the shortest distance between two points. The mind is the same. The mind can tolerate comfortably, only one thing at a time. Instead of multi-tasking and complicating the lives we lead, if we simply do one thing at a given time being fully aware, we can most definitely accomplish all what we need to accomplish in a shorter time. (i.e. 'One thing at a time and that done well').

The tension and stress levels are low when we do only one thing at a time. There is a huge job satisfaction when we do that. Until we were six years old we did that. Unfortunately as we grew older we got more and more complicated. The knots we tie ourselves into are so difficult to untie and unravel. Some may need to be carried over to the next life as well. The recipe is to simplify our lives and make life straightforward, and do everything you do with a smile. And to do each task with full mindfulness - slowly, mindfully and silently!

11. In the Sinhala book on 'Sakman Bhāvanā' it is said that you can combine breath meditation with walking meditation. But when doing this a lot of thoughts keep flowing in. How should a yogi deal with this?

When walking we only focus on the lower part of the body, the legs, feet and ankles. When sitting we focus on the upper part of the body, keeping the lower part still. When sitting we observe the air element and its rubbing/striking feature (*vāyo phoṭṭahba dhātu*) as the draft of air moves in and out of the nostril scraping the nose or the abdomen. When walking we observe the foot making contact with the ground and the ensuing movement. When sitting we keep our mind still, only focusing on the in/out breath or the abdomen. When walking and taking left/right steps, we shift our mind focus to two places, one after the other.

Although we develop mindfulness in both types of meditation, we use two methods to do so. As the yogi keeps walking in this way, they cultivate the ability to turn their mind inwards, and not focus on external matters. Mindfulness becomes firm and turned into the body. In walking, the yogi will note that the mindfulness which first started with the soles of the feet gradually moves upwards, from the ankles, calf, legs and thighs right up to the neck and head. They will note this ascent very well, like in a train when an engine shunts, the vibrations move along the railway carriages one by one in sequence. Therefore even though the attention of the yogi is on the sole of the foot or ankle, mindfulness develops the power to move upwards in stages. This is a positive after effect of the first stages of walking.

Similarly, together with walking, the breathing, the heart beat and all other pulsatile movements can work together with the movements of the feet. For this to happen the yogi should have been walking for about 15 minutes. At such a stage, they may be able to incorporate breath meditation into walking.

Ven Nānārama advised not to use *ānāpānasati* together with walking at the beginning. After commencing walking, if mindfulness sets in well and *samādhi* gets established, then it is appropriate to incorporate breathing. In this situation, *ānāpānasati* is only a secondary object to walking. One can use two similes to explain this technique – first, it would be like a bull, the horns appear after the ears (always the ears appear first). Or when traveling in a car peacefully, we will first establish mindfulness and then later start *ānāpānasati*. Always establish what we started with (e.g. walking) and then move to the secondary object.

12. ***Please advise on walking meditation, whether we contemplate on 'left, right' initially but later move to 'lifting, moving, placing'. Please can you advise the technique that you use?***

According to a famous joke amongst Burmese monks, certain teachers used to ask their pupils to not fail to practice what they preach. But they also ask them to not follow what they practice. Similarly in my personality, my methods of walking meditation are totally different from what I teach. You would not want to emulate me in that regard. I do walking meditation very fast and in a very unorthodox manner. This may be due to my athletic nature.

But the important point is that firstly, walking meditation is common to both *samatha* and *vipassanā* practitioners. Secondly, to all new comers my advice is to start by noting the feet moving as; left-right, left-right. If the yogi notices the hardness/softness of the ground, or the coolness/ heat while practicing in this way, the teacher during the interview will gauge that the yogi is actually veering towards *vipassanā* practice (or *samatha*). If the yogi is more towards s*amatha* the teacher will then encourage the yogi to keep going in this manner repeatedly. Instead, if the teacher concludes that the yogi's tendencies are towards *vipassanā,* he will then advise the yogi to break each step into two, namely; lifting-dropping. Once that is mastered he will be instructed accordingly to note three phases/or notings per step, namely; lifting, moving, placing – in each of the left and right step.

If the mindfulness is stronger the *vipassanā* yogi can go even deeper and contemplate the elements in each step, such as the hardness or coolness of the ground when placing the foot. This is the typical Burmese technique, of three stages. The *Visuddhimagga* goes into six stages. According to the Burmese *vipassanā* method once the noting of physical three steps is mastered the yogi is instructed to observe the intention (*nāma dhamma),* i.e., intention to lift and lifting, followed by the intention to move and moving, followed by the intention to place and placing. This would include intention - *nāma dhamma* as well as *rūpa dhamma.* If the yogi moves fast during that advanced way of noting, they tend to lose balance and sway to and fro, this would mean that the pace of change of position has exceeded their limits of concentration. They will then be advised to revert back to one step. Which means to note lifting and placing only. The teacher will need to then alter the method to suit the individual yogi. This is some brief advice for the time being.

This is true *vipassanā* practice. On the other hand the *samatha* practitioner will only engage in the left/right practice and that is adequate since he does walking meditation purely to get concentration.

Abbreviations

AN	*Anguttara Nikāya*
DN	*Digha Nikāya*
ICU	*Intensive Care Unit*
MN	*Majjhima Nikāya*
SN	*Samyutta Nikāya*

Printed in Poland
by Amazon Fulfillment
Poland Sp. z o.o., Wrocław